WHERE DEATH GOES

WHERE DEATH GOES

POEMS

(9/20/2001 – 5/1/2002)

Daniel Abdal-Hayy Moore

The Ecstatic Exchange

2009

Philadelphia

For quotes any longer than those for critical articles and reviews,
contact:
The Ecstatic Exchange,
6470 Morris Park Road, Philadelphia, PA 19151-2403
email: abdalhayy@danielmoorepoetry.com

First Edition
ISBN: 978-0-578-01084-7 (paper)
Published by *The Ecstatic Exchange*,
6470 Morris Park Road, Philadelphia, PA 19151-2403

The poems *The Egypt Series,* and *Up in the Air (Continuing the Egypt Series)*
appear in the web magazine, *Celestial Graffiti,* as part of the Ira Cohen
Akashic Project

Also available from *The Ecstatic Exchange:*
Knocking from Inside, by Tiel Aisha Ansari

Cover collage by the author
Back cover photograph by Peter Sanders

بسم الله الرحمن الرحيم

DEDICATION

To
Shaykh ibn al-Habib
(and the continuation of the Habibiyya)
Shaykh Bawa Muhaiyuddeen,
all shuyukh of instruction and ma'arifa
and
Baji Tayyaba Khanum

❋

The earth is not bereft
of Light

CONTENTS

AUTHOR'S INTRODUCTION

Left Unfinished at Death...

I don't know if there are any pithy statements, elegant or profound, or any religious teachings that may totally eradicate our anxious curiosity about our own deaths. Though there may be levels of serenity and submission to the fact, and some (absolutely non neurotic) saints of certainty may anticipate their natural deaths with joy, for the most of us, even bolstered by a strong belief system, death for us personally is rather inconceivable, and even a source of wondrous dread. And except for those blessed ones who have truly passed through it, the death of the ego or the self is a tantalizing conundrum posing the question: but after such a death, *what's left?*

Our first glimpse of a dead person is enough to sober our hold on life, as I experienced with a step-grandfather before I was a teenager. He was German-American, and always came to holiday dinners with scrumptious apple pies, and kidded me endlessly about hating beets (which I've since overcome), and now after a brief illness there he was in his coffin, lying in white satin, artificially pink-cheeked, hair combed just so, lifeless.

In an important way death is the bread and butter of poets, and at the heart of all great poems is a consciousness of death, that great energizer toward lively inspiration. Shivered into a realization of our mortality, the poetic impulse is to enunciate our life in all the musical fullness of its textures before it is gone. But death always seems to happen to someone else, and while we may make peace with the fact of it, I'm sure everyone is uncomfortable with the possibility of a disastrous death, an accidental death, a sudden death when we haven't prepared ourselves for it, and hope instead for a nice deathbed death, surrounded by family and beloved friends, in not too much pain, able to deliver kind last words and wise admonitions.

Spanish poet Garcia Lorca wasn't accorded such a death. He was marched out in the middle of the night by the Guardia Civil to an empty area in the local woods and shot. Hart Crane, whether he changed his mind once he hit the water or not, threw himself off the side of a steamer into the sea. World history is studded with astonishingly brutal as well as heroic deaths, as well as some pointless deaths and wholesale and tragically genocidal deaths.

But saintly deaths are something else. In all the human spiritual paths there are stories of great men and women of divine gnosis who die in states of exaltation, sweet relief, or harmonious blending with the Next World that is more of a pause, almost a whisper. And their deaths, while entering holy silence, bring into stronger emphasis their erstwhile presence among people as teachers and examples of true humanity and sincere piety, as if their own lives are proof-positive of God's merciful existence, and their deaths simply a continuing chapter in the Great Adventure.

Perhaps in the core of each person's being, from Tierra del Fuego to the Aleutian Islands, on all points of the human compass, there is a seed of consciousness of this kind of divine death, a way of following death itself, with patience and peace, to where death itself as an entity goes. And in every society there surely exist human souls who have indeed "passed beyond death," the death of the ego or the "self" as it is usually defined by experience, and entered in their lives into a truly balanced and saintly state of equanimity and even vision and miracle, having died to their own selves "unto God," however that may be defined, and having by that grace traded our limited human dimension to God's own dimension of "close friendship," as saints in Islam are called: *Friends of God*.

Now this book of poems was not begun as a sustained meditation on death per se, and the title I was given at its inception (I always seem to begin a book of poems with an evocative title mysteriously given) was *Left Unfinished at Death*. But perhaps it had a bit too much of a fated possibility to retain, and in itself was too superstitiously scary for me to contemplate, so it was changed to simply *Where Death Goes*. And with that formulation death becomes as if a personification of the death state, and with some poignancy has a "place to go" itself that certainly includes us but is without guile or any sense of mortal vindictiveness (as if death in the abstract has some bone to pick with us?). This formulation not being exactly as the personification of the traditional Angel of Death, which as a Muslim I might expect to see come before me to forecast my actual death, but with something of that emotive coloring, a kind of vulnerable, neutral non-being, into whose embrace we are finally swept or into whose non-being we at last most harmoniously flow. Or, as the final title poem's last stanza has it:

> Yet death *goes*
> and takes us with it
> and leaves a Polaroid on an upturned glass
> full of sunset glow for those left behind to
> ponder
>
> And sings a soft song
> as it sinks below the horizon

January 30, 2009

✵

O, Light of my eyes,
They took me from myself today,
Let festivities be prepared,
My golden skinned,
My silver bodied,
My tongue, my beloved has come.
— *Rumi*

SKY HAS MEANING

Sky has meaning by what's passing through it
it means a flock of starlings in bird formation

a *thwap* in space as they head for a hundred distant tree branches
it means a high tower of geometrically arranged

magnolia petals transported on a gilded car by
glistening Indonesians on their way to a green riverbank

it means airplanes grinding high
toward their New York destination bull's eye

it means light like a door's just been flung open down the hall
and light upon light has illuminated the air

coming upon us ever closer like the breath of
death as if closing in on us

but it's not black and claustrophobic it's
like silver circus horses in parallel formation

circling a ring straddled by an ecstatic standing blond in sequins with a
tiny whip shouting out encouraging phrases to no one in particular

her blond tresses snapping in the sky like
audible writing like crisp greetings from the Unseen

like an angelic reminder of the meaning of our lives

we get up from the rubble and walk forward
already dead

we have no need to say goodbye to anyone
everyone else is already dead as well

9/20

THE ELEGANT SHOEMAKER

The elegant shoemaker who knows how to shape the
leather just so and how to
sew the top to the bottom just so
puts down his last and cries

The microbiologist who can spot things through her
microscope no one else sees and how they will
interact with other things in other biological environments
pushes away from the marble-topped lab table and
puts her face in her hands
her sobs echo slightly though the metal-clad laboratory is
crowded

The billionaire computer manufacturer stares out his
high rise window for a moment with
tears in his eyes

The car mechanic black with grease pushes himself out from
under his tenth car today with
grief-stricken face accentuated by oil smudges

Everything is different when east becomes west
and a handkerchief folded in the front jacket pocket
becomes a flag filled with explosives
when doormen suddenly become doors
when the sky becomes a pool volatile stones are skipped in
crosswalks are filled with zoo animals
flame is ignited by writing the name of a loved one
on a scrap of paper no bigger than an ant's antenna

The location of grief is a town filled with dead firemen

The location of grief is at the intersection of
rage and bewilderment

I've seen elephants recognize long-lost friends by entwining their
trunks and trumpeting like God's own thunders
but the drop of grief that hangs on the faucet and
won't fall down the drain or on a
dew-drenched branch at dawn before the deer have
entered the meadow
or on the eyelashes of the two-year-old who suddenly realizes
her mother's not lost after all in the supermarket she's just
turned her back for a moment to reach for a multicolored cereal box
or a black shroud of grief so
great that it covers all the shoppers at once…

I leave this unfinished at death
the moonlight is already unzipping the hills
and diving into its delicious love affair with
the night

The windows this high up above the city are
filling with dove cutouts at acute angles
upward

It levels out from here
all the way to the sea

But a funny car comes to collect us
standing in our white raincoats facing the

wind
each of us clutching the pencil that might have
put the finishing touches on everything
if our time hadn't run out

or more specifically our time hadn't made a
subtle transition into another sphere of an altogether
different space and a more glorious activity
where moon-sized facial expressions and
gestures more like dancing take over from our
deliberate lives into the
methodology of music

the strategy and counter-strategy of complete silence

the hush of fresh water over sharp rock
soothing our hearts

9/27

A FIRE-BREATHING DRAGON

A fire-breathing dragon has come to live with us
and except for incinerating the furniture he's
an exemplary guest
doing as fire-breathing dragons do

We have a hard time hearing conversations when he's
in our midst because of the very great
volume of bellowing oven-sound like a factory specializing in
things molten say rather than
a quiet assembly line where tops are screwed down

The dragon opens its mouth to add a
word or two or even to yawn if it's a bit
past his naptime
and the couch catches fire the print of one of
Turner's seascapes ignites and the sound as of an
inferno drowning out all other sound
consumes both words and their innermost meanings

He brought his friend the Tyger of Wrath one day
who sat fairly still considering but who when
spoken to would go all red and roar one of those
especially hair-raising tiger roars that seem to
get louder and more

ferocious and never end and it's like the
tiger's fallen in love with the sound of his own roaring and is
encouraged by it to roar all the
louder and seemingly forever

and if the dragon gets into it we generally have to
exit the house altogether and start looking for
new quarters since the old one's now

wrapped in all-embracing flame and totally
engulfed in a rapture of singing fire whose
words we can faintly make out in the
black night as we stand in our
only clothes with pale clouds
scudding overhead and more than likely a full moon
the night so still

and red embers flying upward into the
yawning star-lit void the planets quietly spinning in their
safe distance
and the words we can make out go something like

Let it all go it's gone anyway before you even get a
good grip on it it's water now being
evaporated into steam it's wood now being
incinerated into ash it's air blowing flames into
ever-greater life it's soul enrapturing soul-essence
whose eyes are ablaze with one of the
highest forms of love but whose

recipients may take a lifetime to
recognize it as such

Let the fiery sparks fall
into intelligent patterns around you they'll
spell out the deft particularities of this

song they'll

bless your mortality with the wisdom of fire
they'll wrap you in it after all

and make you flame

9/28

I WOULD ENSHRINE THE SALMON

I would enshrine the salmon leaping upstream against
horrendous odds and tons of crashing water

or the mighty butterfly migrations flapping their wings not only
to the southern tip of Brazil but back again

I'd immortalize the heroic human gesture the extended hand the
soothing word in a catastrophe

except that they're already pumped with the
divine light they had at their inception

the kind word to a sad child the haircut for an
invalid

the fly let out the screen door rather than crushed
the voice of calm at the center of a wildfire capable of

eating through acres of forest in one fiery bite
and burping out a blackened wasteland for miles under

hosannas of smoke
deep inside where shut eyes go where the central place is

when the eyes can't take any more
physical seeing and must cover their pinpoint pupils with

a flesh lid until all's become black

Deep inside there once the remove has been made
somewhat complete

shines the enshrined moment of grace its absolute essence
where divine strands hang down and another sweeter

light altogether augments the scene
and salmon leap in their own Paradise

and sing

10/5

THE HORN OF PLENTY

The horn of plenty and the trumpet of doom
the Bells of St. Marys and *For Whom the Bell Tolls*
The Black Stallion and *The Four Horsemen of the Apocalypse*
what a thin line between plenty and penury
thirst and thrust
Hershey and Hiroshima

One moment breathing
the next moment bone
one moment singing the next moment stone
hilarity into sterility
gaiety into anxiety
skating into scattering
stuttering into stating the case clearly

O dearly beloveds we are gathered together
we are tarred and feathered
by the side of the grave of the world
where the angel of death comes
when we are most alive
where we are lost but arrive
at certainty before our eyes
shovel into lovely
hurt into dirt
light into light itself
transformed into light

10/7

BEGUN BY THE LIGHT OF THE MOON

Begun by the light of the moon
reflected off the wall of a barn
black horse silhouette in the gloom
by the gush of a nearby stream

Begun when the night is strange
and strangeness seems to take hold
of the few material forms
and transfigures them into gnome-shapes
or slithering incorporeal forms
lit by an inner glow

So that what by day is a fence becomes
a procession of wavering shades
or the tree that has daily stood tall
on that hill for the last hundred years
silently screams like a banshee from hell
as rag clouds scuttle and disperse

Begun when the world is raw
and its elements between taking shape and dissolving
somewhere between waking and sleep
that dry ocean of tumultuous currents
that green highway like virgin grass in moonlight
that Technicolor chasm of imponderable wonders

A life begun and its meanings arising
like incipient words in a decipherable sentence
left unfinished at death

an utterance begun in the liquid season
but left incompletely congealed
a song begun in the back of the throat in the
pitch black unknown part of the heart
and even in the body's unknowable wellsprings

Begun in a whisper millennia old
left floating like a phrase only faintly overheard
or like words pronounced on lips that will
pronounce no more words forever
as they lapse into bone

10/15

SOULS

There are so many souls worth saving
the face wreathed in roses whose eyes tell tales from
before civilization when trees were sturdy giant ferns cut from
crystal

The grandmother with ten white horses on a steep green hillside
whose middle name is a secret she calls on to heal
the cut finger the burnt tongue the earache the limp
the mental hesitation

The twelve old men from the remote mountain village
all brothers from the same mother and father
all twelve so filled with natural goodness and so
physically alike the townspeople call each one of them
Joseph

So many Lord on this raw earth of sharp ice and
wild flame saw teeth and soft rollers

The shy schoolteacher in the ghetto
who smuggles her paycheck money into various lunchboxes

The girl of six who stands up for the boy in class who peed his pants
against the taunts of the others

The fireman who hears a cry and suddenly sees
the Celestial City shimmering through columns of flame
and walks through them to his Lord
Lord the cries of endurance and laughter of terror

these human souls You fashion out of
red dust and divine breath on a
mountaintop we may never see
then lay them into wombs and later into
tombs to be assembled before You on that Awesome Day

No cranes cross a bronze sky

No dust mote floats in the still air

And our souls stand out like diamonds on black velvet

Like trumpets in a library

10/18

THEY ALL WENT SOUTH FOR THE WINTER

They all went south for the winter
leaving the branches bare and the crags empty

the colorful plumage of the air the darting sprays of feathery sparks
gone for the duration of the

barren season
moonlight looking down now on

dry fields and overgrown tombs
mirrors hardly catching a reflection before

letting it go
doorways hardly framing a body before it

vanishes from its rectilinear confines into an
oblivion of rooms and an absolute invisibility of space

Names elude their owners becoming instead a way of
forgetting a face and the stories it might recall

all its accumulation of past gestures winks smiles widening
or the embarrassed lowering of the eyes

Now geese go out across slate green fields
squawking their *sayonaras* to the reeds and croaking toads

ice cracks in glasses on abandoned shelves
a pewter sun meekly lights scrub trees and broken roofs

barn doors hang open like lazy mouths

But a cocoon in a dusty corner contains all the
renewal the world needs for its

grasses to blow bright green in an ignited sun
and a cobweb between twigs to catch fresh

flies who contain all the seasons within them
as the spider feels the twitch along his guy-wire that will

bring gold again to the fields and
set glorious flames of flowers burning in broad daylight

as the divine shadow passes across the sky

10/23

LITTLE SLIP OF DELICATE FILIGREE LACINESS

Little slip of delicate filigree laciness
of atomic detail in duplicate

carefully patterned in perfect geometry
quadruplicate multiplied actual-size infinitely

elaborate jaggedy curvatures and circularities
carefully and ever-so even more ever-so carefully

crafted not by a human hand so deftly
but spun from breath into form that stands

brilliantly against the illusion of nothingness when everything
meshes ever-so cunningly and star-like in dazzle sends light

directly and diagonally into every corner of what's known
definitely as well as what's not known in ignorance blissfully

the dot that expands to the size of the Milky Way
and tilts full of star-debris like dust from a

spring cleaning of sky-carpets shaken in every space living room
simultaneously but then telescoped down into

microscopic diddle-piddly so confounding so utterly beyond what
language can adequately describe in detail or

express exactly to correspond even myopically with what's
real in reality of this

infinite laciness this tenderest cordiality of heart-to-heart
plurality as well as unique as diamond individuality

Nothing is itself alone but sustained by God's
breath in such breath-bursts and breath-forms we're

swept away utterly and left
gasping here stuttering our whole bodies

quivering as if the earth itself had been suddenly
metamorphosed into a transparency

and was melting gigantically and
heroically into a single heartbeat that

would transport us directly and immediately out of our
material vicinity into what can only be

hinted at as pure irradiating and ever-more blindingly irradiating
divinity

10/24

SEVERAL SWEET PURPLE TENDRILS

Several sweet purple tendrils in little
ribbony curdles

untwisted above the wreckage by day or by
night some thought it was smoke from the

gas fuel fires some thought it was the
evil mist of it or the dust from the workers

everyone had an opinion as the tendrils continued to
write out their lazy message over and over to

no one by day or by night in the dark or by
daylight like fingers threading through weave to make a

tangible wall hanging or calligraphy of the
flip side of reality the rough side the side left always

unfinished unpresentable a few stray
hairs a few flying threads

an echo in space a reverberation from the initial
godly shout the initial *fiat* of command that makes all things

stand at attention at last and go from practically
nothing at all to a squall over the Pacific a

tsunami higher than a hundred of the highest
skyscrapers a vantage of interior vision greater than

any saint living in this dimension or the next
several sweet purple tendrils in little

ribbony curdles
tirelessly signing as if to the deaf

from the utter silence of matter

from the universe contemplating its own disasters

from the twisting wisps of light left by God

above the chessboard Alma Mater

in His inaudible lottery

10/27

CHINESE RESTAURANT

for Tom Buckner and Kamala Cesar

I'm alone in a Chinese Restaurant in New York *The*
Ginger House on Fashion Avenue favorite of my dear friends
Tom and Kamala and I expect when I look down into my
bowl of noodles to see an ivory palace with delicate
filigree portico surrounded by miniature
cypress trees and a teeny-tiny elderly couple in silk robes
with wisps of blue steam rising from their
syllables gently looking up at me and waving with
long sleeves no hands showing

and when I sip the orange-brown tea from the
white cup I imagine I'll see a reflection of those dramatic
cliffs as if blown by giant hurricanes rising
majestically in slate gray and blue-green into a
white sky filled with even whiter cranes flying in loose formation

And now I'm on the New Jersey Transit to Trenton
and I expect to see the deposed king of Tortola Land or
Leopoldville
heralded by three tall whippets on diamond leashes and he
walks down the aisle like an ermine-clad James Brown
followed by faithful retainers in this
humble train of blue collar workers and tired
New York shoppers and families with newborns

He'd be on Amtrak eating lobster croissants except that like
us he's on a tight budget these days and even the

ermine isn't real the diamonds fake the whippets actually emaciated
poodles

Soon I'll be out on the street in Philadelphia
and I expect to see the last horse-drawn carriage the
final politician's funeral cortège through
cobbled streets the Old City pulling down its
corrugated doors for the night

And within this bedraggled domain I expect to see
a glory surrounding our heads and hearts
with miniature golden race-horses charging to the
uttermost ends of its rays
and saints in work clothes and aprons
touching the lame and the homeless with
beneficent touch

and the faces of innocent zoo animals floating for a
moment in the air to show our inseparability from all
living creatures each of whom must
eat to live

just as I ate my tofu and vegetables on rice at *The
Ginger House* at the beginning of this poem
when the table was bare and like these
pages before I began writing

was covered with clean white paper in sweet
preparation for the meal

10/28

APPROACH THE RIM OF A VOLCANO

Approach the rim of a volcano
notice its molten ruby cast
the fiery frothing restlessly of roiling spew
walk a little closer to the grate of Hell
and look down past the flimsy iron bars and note
how redder how hotter how angrier and ready to

Well I've lost interest in describing it any further
it's past my bedtime and past my
powers of description or perhaps I just don't
want to believe in Hell I just want to believe in
grottoes of ivy-clinging rock walls and fountains so
crystalline and plentiful at every turn and in
every vista

Let Hell burn in its own fires
let its roar be muffled in my ears

but authorities better than I warn that it's near
and won't be ignored when the body's spirit is
loosed into its native world
and the pendulum hung from unfathomably high
swings way back this way to show the cool snows and
green valleys of bliss's endlessness

and then swings way forward to reveal
the atomic migraine the bone-crushing endless cancerous
neuralgia of Hell without letup
and our souls nudged toward the

pendulum's judicial slice forever into either
one or the other

10/30

THE TALLEST BUILDING IN NEW YORK

My aunt Agatha's name is Eleanor and her
emblem is a roaring rhinoceros on a lilypad

Blue trees growing under the skin all bloom simultaneously
their flowers are handkerchiefs

Soap sails across the sky on the bubbles it makes at contact with
the air though scientists don't know why but are
investigating the phenomenon by sitting on
lawn chairs in Honolulu reading Melville in Chinese

The light of the full moon is a tumbler full of marbles on a
shelf of alabaster in a house of glass the shape of a
cuckoo clock

This is a poem of irrationalities leading to a punch line

The Empire State Building is again the tallest building in New York

The Empire State Building is again the tallest building in New York

The Empire State Building is again the tallest building in New York

11/3

A GLASS FISH

A glass fish served on a glass platter on a
glass table in a glass house

a treatise on paper written on paper and
printed on paper in a paperback read by a paperboy on his

paper route
a tree within a tree within a tree within a

sliver in a finger making it twitch involuntarily
the universe ball in the shape of a giant hole surrounding an

invisible ball because it's incorporeal and
drifts along the ceiling of the world like a

phantom whispering the Name of the Lord over and
over on incandescent lips which is also

the celestial engine that makes it move
across from one wall to another and

ultimately out the door left open by godly
accident to mosey along out in the air over

fields of field mice among wheat fields and
cornfields where each ear is silver and each

kernel a diamond so that the
glitter is blinding

which makes no real difference since our
eyes are closed above the

mouth that eats
the mouth that stays shut

the mouth that sings such songs as these to

gnats and spiders listening in the halls and
adding to their seductive repertoire even

mites whose prophet's name escapes me at the moment
but who move with mite mightiness in a

mite's world suited and created
specifically for mites

11/5

STARTLED AWAKE

for Farouq Abi

Startled awake by a loud clanging noise
or by the soft rustle of a teeny-tiny worm underground

or by the screeching brakes of a hundred-mile-an-hour locomotive
or by the first whirrs of a baby gnat's wing taking to the air

or by the sudden crash of a tidal wave sounding like a herd of rogue
elephants plowing into a beach

or by the rosy dawn coming up over the hills inch by
pale inch like the sound of a

butterfly's wings fanning above an abyss

or by the deep bass sound of the abyss itself simply being an abyss
mysterious and deep

startling us awake by the very concavity of this
existence whose every whirling atom like a

zillion delirious tops on slick reflective marble
spinning in a zillion different dimensions and reflected between

sun and moonlight infinitely out into space in a zillion glittering facets
startles us awake to stagger ecstatic down the

dark hall until it becomes bright as

heaven on a Friday morning when the

clouds have been brushed and beaten clean
and our hearts are aloft on the soft sound of their

own beating
God breathing His own Name into their beating

like larks' wings in angular flocks over a
sleeping city whose sudden takeoff like an eyelid bursting open

startles us awake

11/7

CHILDREN OF THE ANTS

Children of the ants children of the corn kernel
children of the dandelion growing in an orchid patch
children of the shadow of the bridge to the big city
children of truck exhaust and coal dust

children of the ancient lineage
of the mysterious moan in the forest
of the street corner where people have
met their fate and lived to relate it

children of moisture and dryness of plenty and
penury
children whose hearts are a blaze of lights
whose path goes between buildings to a
green openness

children of darkness and nothingness
who've sat at the king's table in borrowed ermines and eaten
chocolate-dipped strawberries and
slivered succulent alabaster fruits
directly with the king
bathed in splattering shafts of the king's light
and returned to town again in sackcloth and
cardboard shoes preceded by donkeys
stuttering when spoken to
incapable of giving directions to the police station
to the woman with the dogs

children of the suspended dust mote in a light shaft

of the shadow of rainbows crossing a rushing stream

children of cows and horses grazing absentmindedly

children of the unknown nuclear physicist riding the subway

children of the cobwebby corner and the inclined plane

children of breadcrumbs blown from God's feast
in a Paradise of eye blinks and an

avalanche of sweet breaths
expelled from His divine lungs into their own

11/9

WE SAT

1

We sat at the base of the dead tree and sang the
wine song until the branches ungnarled and the
leaves pushed out green paddles breast-stroking
the air

Honey appeared on our lips and ran down our chins

Roses appeared all around us as if outlining
our bodies for further investigation

A fresh breeze appeared from the east as if a
window sealed shut from disuse had been
miraculously opened
or as if a neglected love letter sealed shut years ago
and seeming to signal the end of the affair
had been miraculously unsealed and streamers and
live golden birds and visions of otherworldly landscapes were all
floating through the air to us recalling the
everlivingness of love and the utter
singularity of the Beloved

A wall opened to our right looking out on
a desert where tribes of Bedouin sang in giant
circles in the moonlight making divine calligraphy in the sand

A wall opened to our left onto a waterfall so intense
the strands of plummeting water actually created

symphonic music and threw shifting
murals of steam before our eyes depicting
the rise and fall of historical events in the
evanescent vapor form of their
true reality in the first place finally
made plain

But the eyes of the singers of the songs we sang
cast beams before them from the early
forests of their sound
and lit up the rooms we later
occupied long after the songs died away

And the living branches of the tree shook
above our insubstantial roofs both
beautifully and mightily and alive to the
ends of our days

2

We've sat in the open meadow and let
deer nibble on our eyebrows and hair

What's all this light filling the valley with its
elegant poppies whose faces are all imploring us to silence?

What's all this rushing water and atoms
set loose in the world like a whirlwind of dandelions and dust?

It's said it all began with the Word

and from it flow multitudes of words both

fancy and plain that adorn the air with their
songs

A lantern is set on a window ledge and
cutout silhouette shapes of fantastic

animals parade across its mellow golden light

The light flickers and the animals seem to
come alive

Someone shrieks at a lion who seems to
open his mouth

Our shapes appear the same way
but no one shrieks or even catches their breath

Everyone sighs and applauds

The lamplight flickers and we seem to come
alive

but the paper shapes are set aside one on
top of another

and only the lamplight keeps shining

We think if we fall into the lamplight we'll
burn to cinders

It's true that for a while we may assume
the shape of light

When the summer comes the valley fills with
rabbits and foxes

When the snow comes the rabbits disappear into the
blinding whitenesss and the foxes

Slink around with aching stomachs

The wind is carrying messages from God
and sparkles landing on the branches

are punctuation marks periods and
exclamation points that put ecstatic

emphasis on the fall of a leaf or the
watery rustle of a pebble in a stream

Everything proclaims Him
everything sings

Can't you hear everything
repeating His Name?

11/11

THE MAN DIAGNOSED WITH COLON CANCER
WHO'D REFUSED A COLONOSCOPY

The interior of my body is God's territory
I walk on God's earth
He walks on my inner landscape leaving His
delicate dimensionless footprints on my internal organs

seeing His reflection in the glisten of my
kidneys talking with a soft voice into the calliope
chambers of my heart both
left and right ventricles and listening to the
echoes rebound in delirious spirals

sending His angels through my bloodstream swimming the
same way they swim through the open valleys of the stars
with their incandescent wings held back as if
gliding

He peers into the curiously vast
geometries of my brain expanding past their
edges with His incorporeal Presence
like the reverberations of a gong

looks out through my eyes and beholds His
outer territory and all His territories in between
and back again into the outerness of my innermost interior

and sinks back on the pillows of these
miraculously perfect but perishable soft organic
engines He's created and creates with each

breath for our rivering souls to flow in as we sit

remembering or forgetting Him as we stand to leave
or enter another of His rooms

or fall into deep sleep as our outer territory enters into
an interior territory entirely His where

soul gossamer and soul silk and soul crystal
in bodiless vastnesses

momentarily abide

11/12

YOU'LL SING A SONG

You'll sing a song from somewhere out of your depths
and light will hit it and it'll be
a diamond brooch worn at the back of
Layla's head in a sunny glade

It'll be a drop of water hanging at the
tip of a leaf in a dark rainforest radiating diamond light

a deep chasm with a train trestle above it and an
old fashioned train chugging along
oblivious to all danger over a giant arc filled with blue smoke

When you open your heart to sing
the whole room becomes a single ear

or even no ear at all but more like a
sharp point say of a needle about to
enter a cloth to sew
a saintly sleeve to the main body of the divine garment

the exact tip of the needle the sound-receiver receives
for the entire universe made drunk in the
sudden echoing orbit of your song

11/14

THE ALCHEMIST

The alchemist sat in his brass chair
and took the ivory figure of a horse and
set it on the tabletop and it
took off at top speed with a vision in its
eyes no man could fathom

He took the ashes of a rose in the palm of his
hand and set them stem first into the
fresh river water in the tall glass vase that moments before was
just a sketch on paper

He took a gulp of air and sat quite still for a
moment in the middle of a dense forest attended by
stags

He drank a potion that was just rainwater
collected in a trumpet flower
and saw a youth dressed in leaves gazing with
love on everything around him appear for a
moment in his mirror held in his hand above the fire

and he leaned back in his brass chair in the
dark laboratory off Moulton Street smelling of
overheated beakers and things dipped in soot
and sighed and the strange pneumatic song of his
sighs became a garden grove especially for
him filled with gardenias and hibiscus flowers brazenly
extolling God in a voice only the actual
air of the sky could adequately hear

though his own eyes filled with

fresh salty tears when he
heard it

11/20

SEVENTY-THOUSAND OF THEM

Seventy-thousand of them gather on a
gelatinous rim and we can't see
any of them

They glow and glimmer as they rotate nonchalantly through their
life-cycles of flame-out form-making flash-forth of inner
froth then shimmer for a few million

summers sending only furtive and darkish
news from so far away to us on earth
their exasperated lovers longing for more
light than is physically available in order to

move easily into more meaningful realms where our
heartbeats are crowned with glories of liquid pearl and no two
beats are the same anymore but each is a
key to another deep space-embraced
planetary sphere

11/24

HE FELL TO HIS KNEES

He fell to his knees
but the buildings came down

The sky filled with vaporous forms on their
knees in the highest silhouette heavens where the
light is most intense and most pure
but the buildings came down

His heart became spiral staircases leading to
Him
wingéd messengers rushing the steps ten at a time
to deliver his pleas
but the buildings came down

Children fell to their knees at the gates as the
Mongols' horses galloped furiously in
each child gaining years as their
hearts prayed for mothers and grandfathers
but the Mongols invaded
and the entire city came down
all the buildings came down
their prayers with more stirring hooves than the horses
but the buildings came down
their faces dark with a sudden wisdom
but the buildings came down

The violent earthquake threw people to their knees
their prayers stronger than a
million oceans

but the city came down
buildings came crumbling down
their voices rose like iron barricades in the
sky like walls against certain disaster
their eyes focused on heaven their hearts repeated
two or three hammering words over and over
but the buildings came down
they prayed until even their faces crumbled
but the buildings came down

Each trickle of divine compassion poured down

the gorgeous reply more majestic than the
origin of the species more elegant than
the creation of a fern the body's
ability to heal more perfect than a blood cell
or the eye of vision itself

but the buildings came down

the song of deliverance
came down with the dust
as the buildings came down

God's Face in the smoke
as the buildings came down

His Word on lips unfathomable to tell
as the buildings came down

the difficult answer coming down with the buildings

as all the buildings
came down

11/26

THE 23rd POEM

FOR THE 23rd POEM

1

For the 23rd poem I wrote a poem that began
"Why do the dead always move in single file?"

that was in a notebook for this
book of poems called *"Where Death Goes"* the final entry

before two men in the dark of night in sweat shirts with hoods up just
outside our house came up to us on the sidewalk and one asked

"What time is it?" then after some jumpy moves *"Give me your money"*
and I immediately hurled my shoulder bag with all my
might at the one who

said this with my poetry notebook in it and that
one poem not yet typed up that

began with that line then went on to
sort of describe the chronological order of the

dead from their
absolute moment of death from ninety-nine-year-old dowager to

few-months old embryo to Hottentot chieftain to Honolulu ex-hula
dancer to young up-and-coming corporate president of an aneurysm while

presiding over a
merger not realizing he'd also soon be

merging stark naked into the Magnificent Unnamable Swirl
and I started yelling *"Fire!"* at the top of my lungs with all the
possible Pavarotti power I could muster and he unfortunately
caught the bag I'd flung and growled *"Shut up where's the*

money" and I yelled back
"It's in the wallet in the bag but leave the bag it's got my

POETRY IN IT!" which he studiously
ignored taking off with the bag down the

street with his silent and anonymous
buddy me still yelling *"FIRE!"* at top voice hoping to bring the

neighbors out in droves and head him off but to no avail the long street
silent and dark with the two men now running to the corner and me

yelling like crazy

So I'm left with one
poem missing from my prodigious

output one glaring gap in my oeuvre but writing this
down the following night I'm grateful I've still got

live breath in my lungs living light in my eyes God surrounded me with
cool aplomb and powerful bellows realizing in that instant if it was

time for me to die so be it
I yelled *"Fire!"* and continued

yelling it after them as they ran
down the block with my
wallet with sixty dollars credit cards family pictures
dragonfly wings elephant tusks angel faces plus an old wrinkled

Mexican peso and an equally wrinkled Egyptian real tucked into the
billfold and in a bag compartment nail clippers eyeglass repair kit vintage

pocket pencil-sharpener father's heirloom pocket tape measure with his
lifelong company's logo of antique wooden-wheeled truck on it

now lost forever
and the poem continued but I can't really recreate it adequately so it's

also gone as well and for just as long a time
though my own death averted for a moment or two

awaiting its precise chronology in the
mysterious and occasionally seemingly

perverse but actually perfect and divine
scheme of things

2

So these two poor bedraggled black guys who've
got my bag have got one billfold with now
cancelled credit and debit cards and sixty bucks
one poetry notebook one folder with the same poems minus
one typed for easier reading

They're not pushing wheelbarrows of gold coins over a
green hill in Ireland whistling a country reel

they're not digging a djinn's treasure in
Morocco with magic spells protecting them rubies diamonds
untold riches tumbling at their feet

they're not suddenly blessed with perfect
Bodhissatvic enlightenment I don't think but then again
maybe they are and I also thought at
various times during the day they might be
Allah's angels come to divest me of my
attachments I yelled out *"Leave me my poetry notebook"*
like a perfect lunatic who
could've gotten shot through the heart for such
rash stupidity

They're hardly worth fretting over these bewildered probably
drug-addled desperados maybe they lost their
jobs in a machine parts factory
maybe they'll read the poems and get an idea or two like a
cartoon light bulb going off however dimly
they're certainly guardians of the Unseen and
anti-this-world warriors ferociously divesting at least
me and God knows who else of either
a few bits and pieces of material wealth or if they're really desperate
mortality itself may God protect them and us from such
utter desperation

They'll eventually get caught for some stupid something or other
and sit in a piss-smelling cell awaiting

paperwork and lineups harsh lighting and
no earthly comforts or sweetness for a long time
and my bag's no doubt in a bush or down a
drain having done
no good in their hands to anyone

but my hands are free

I look at them and see God's
light shining out from their palms for a
moment

The death path forsook me

3

Let them sail on the high seas with pirates
dance around gypsy bonfires to accordions and tambourines
don't let them be treated like the lowlifes they are Lord
let them have adventures at least befitting men
not squatting on some jail toilet in full view
but riding Mongolian horses down hills on village
raids like righteous thieves at least

I fear the gnarled declensions of their souls
the knotted darkness that twists their lives like
dirty washing that never twists dry

those blasted buggers who stole my bag
give them the open sea or the

pampas of the gauchos instead of a
cramped and crowded sweaty bus with
bars on the windows to pick up
garbage alongside the highway

Why do the dead always move in single file?
why is each wave of the sea a single individual folded in the
perpetuity of the whole?

Why did I walk away from the encounter unscathed while the
perpetrators are left with their unsatisfied aggression?

The German magistrate who died surrounded by
grandchildren followed by the Australian Aborigine who
fell from a rock followed by the teenager in the
car crash followed by the saint who smiled at the
descending light until it landed on her
lips at the last minute to spell out the

marvelous continuation of the world each one in

perfect step formation each leaf each

microbe in single file forever

from here on out until the

end of time

CODA

And then walked away

Put the mouse in his house and the cheese on the
dish

and then walked away

Sat the old man down very carefully to tea

and then walked away

Put the dress on the rack and the hanger on the
rod and

then walked away

Brought the newborn baby into the world
slapped its puckered bottom and kissed its
wet red face

and then walked away

Sat at the edge of the raging volcano

and then walked away

Took the anonymous hand reaching out from the
rubble and then

walked away

Wiped a tear blew a nose brushed back a hair
watched a sunset rowed a boat walked
through ten burning houses

and then walked away

Saw the angel and conversed over a pure
glass of milk a globe of light the
size of a microbe and

then walked away

Saw the globe of light expand past the
dimension of air

and then walked away

Saw the air expand past the confines of space

and then walked away

Met death face to face as it fumbled for its gun

and then walked away

12/11-13

THE PERFECT PRICE

1

The perfect price for the things we do
circulates through angelic stations like a wheel
with candles on the inside circumference lit and kept alight through
each revolution while starlight on the outer circumference
shatters the darkness with intense incandescent shafts
and equal amounts of ecstatic song

each window we open in a dark house
each spider we wink at when the broom leaves its
web intact each word like a sliver of soap sent to
another through bars of a dank prison on a steep hill

the confounded confabulations of our
own knotted crossroads like the harsh symptoms of an
ancient curse uttered aloud and reverberating all the
way to here

I sing that starry candled wheel out of
circumstances beyond our control sending it on its
upward road

the utterly vulnerable humanity of us wiping our
own mouths with the tattered napkins of our
own souls in a windy place barely
holding on and made as
one-dimensional as possible by this world when in purest
actuality there are a

thousand million voices in our voice and the light of a
thousand million universes in the lights of our
eyes and each gesture of ours conscious or
unconscious takes in Tibet with its intricate icons
and the warm open currents of Caribbean seas

our bodies themselves perfect or deformed by the
slightest or greatest flaw inward or
outward like a pantheon of mythological beings waiting to be
called from the wings to perform in a
grand classical tragicomedy accompanied by
choruses and tympani and the clear
angelic trumpets of ideal musical undercurrents flowing
directly from overlapping seas of
love in latitudes beyond all our mortal fathomings

2

Like the lily the form of whose liquid petals only
divine geometry knows
how it will flute out at the end of its stem and
hang its bee-platform into space at just such an
angle at just such a tilt in the clear air

or how the winds will blow on a certain day at a
certain hour when all was perfectly still a moment before
suddenly leaves and branches torn and sent
flying like angry love letters across unpredictable
distances

or like what we will do and how we will
do it when we've sat up in bed and put our
feet squarely on the floor again for another
episode of mobility in this world whose
edges and corners actually
jut out into the next
and whose windows and air-currents actually
open out onto untold vistas of the Unseen

this world huddled up against the next in the divinely
drenched molecular rainfall of barely
substantial materiality that supposedly sets this world
off from the next when it's more like an
interrupted extension from one world to
another one breath from this side through death to the
other side where radiant splashes are oceanically
greater and travel between stars soaked in
spectacular starlight is made
infinitely easier

and far easier to understand
are the deepest messages
in the meanings we receive

12/17

IN THE NIGHT

In the night I had achieved soft moosehood
getting through the bathroom door was no mean feat
and speaking of feet I now had a hundred
so that I had to check from waist down to make sure
I weren't no centipede thank you Kafka
but my heart was intact Lord be praised and that was as
always platters of recently peeled kiwi fruits and leeched cashews
and interconnecting blue pools up silvery hillsides much
frequented by flamingos

Living the rest of my life this way however
was a bit of a puzzle
what to say to friends on the phone before actually
meeting since my
voice was the same and gave no
indication whatsoever that any
major change had occurred

What to do with the wings was also problematic
although they fit nicely under their twin shell-like
back-pack cases when not in service

I thought perhaps I was dreaming all this
except that I had woken up not
fallen asleep

When I went to the mirror my hundred little
rippling legs carrying me and dodging the
doorframe by tilting my great antlers sideways

lo and behold! I was the
same as always
normal in every way

well maybe not

inwardly I'd turned into vast
wilderness area in Saskatchewan

12/20

THE REASON

Imagine you're walking in a rose garden
time's become strangely irrelevant as if you were just like those
streams of water in a waterfall pouring down a
side into a foaming pool then lying
placid in the sun simply floating in its basin
and strolling now between rose bushes you're lying
placid in the sun calmly eddying
with no particular forward motion though not at all
static or completely motionless but instead kind of
contentedly awake letting the sun's
light and heat fall on you as you walk

rows upon rows of carefully tended roses
some with velvety deep purple inside their petals' folds
some with almost a crisp white-yellow fringe at their
edges while the rest of the rose is a palely
glowing orangey-pink

The garden goes up a hill though the
rose grove is in a level glade
and you notice suddenly some of the roses are in the
shapes of little houses with peaked roofs
others are in the shapes of nineteenth century schooners
equipped with rigging and sails
others have faces and look up at you as you
pass with moist red eyes as if they've been
weeping or reading

others are splayed open and their petals are

spiraling to the ground and you see the entire
bush is in motion or the entire
world and everything is swirling
faster than you could imagine around the
still point of the actual center of the
rose you are gazing into

and above us the sky is opening its petals as well
and light is angling through the curved corridors the
petals make with their translucent bowls
and at the center of the sky around which the entire
universe is streaming

is the invisible rose you came into this
rose garden to see and whose growth and
blossoming is the reason that every day you
come here
to see it

12/22

THE HONING OF A HARMONICA

The honing of a harmonica to a single note
but a single perfect note many birds could perch on
comfortably before taking off to Tahiti
or at least where small red berries grow on tangible branches
while snow falls unceasingly on Buffalo

The clarification of all our cries to a single cry
all our dissuasions and hesitations that make us
fall back like shadows from the high illumination of the
thing itself
of the light of God in all His humor and gravity
a cry nurtured into almost song long and pure enough for
a gaggle of migrating geese to fly over casting a
rapid shadow in the Y-form of a *Yes* affirming the
acceptance to the next world of souls

The deepening of our heartbeats to an almost
audible bass line under every rock'n'roll action of ours
through doors up escalators in the dark privacy of our
most introspective rooms
melted into that which is greater than itself by
dimensional leaps so that one beat is the
Grand Canyon on a sunny day with sky writing of
luminous clouds above
the next beat is the depth of the ocean God's own
breathing metronomes into unceasing increase and decrease

We link to the dark parts as well as the light
encompassed in a sonic boom articulated to our

auditorium ears alert even to the most distant
passing of meteors

as they streak from darkness to darkness in a lightburst like the

sudden ecstatic recognition of

His Name

12/29

THE ANIMAL THAT WE ARE

Suppose the animal that we are got
suddenly transformed into pure spirit
losing our hangnails our dandruff our wrinkles
in exchange for a translucence that could
light up a dark street on the
seedy side of town

and millions of tiny fluttering wings sprouted on all our
extremities even on our
tongues in the invisible realm so that
every word of ours could essentially be sung to a
faraway tune made near by the
haunting familiarity of its notes
as if taught to us by our mothers in the womb

which in fact it was but taught by God alone

Suppose all the gnarled temptations all the
trepidations and hesitations of our
bodies suddenly vaporized and we could
walk in the world as if
passing through water
remembering all the most profound things
thoughts treatises theological disputations that in
every case would lead to actual
face to face knowledge of
God's radiance down to the smallest microbiological hair

Trees lose their flame-like vulnerability

rocks lose their stubborn blank-faced solidity
air itself with all its light is more like our bodies
and light itself even more so
interpenetrating our beings to their immaterial cores
and our beings flowing directly to their
source like the highest notes possible to sing

the takeoff of a flock of egrets
from the silvery surface of a
marsh in moonlight

a sound like angelic applause

a silence from the other side
made suddenly audible in our flesh

through the dazzling wattage of our blood

1/1

AN OLD COUPLE

An old couple sitting in the deli still in their
overcoats and hats each
reading a newspaper

He becomes involved in international diplomacy
rides into the fray in black limousine flanked by
motorcycles and appeases both sides astonishingly by his cool aplomb

She's editing her collected papers for the
Anthropological Society on Social and Exotic
Culinary Customs Among the Hottentots

They turn their pages and take
sips from their cappuccinos

He gazes momentarily at the underwear ads then goes on to
the situation in the Philippines
the air heating up around him the mosquitoes and
tropical bird cries and cracks of nearing rifle fire

She's entertaining grandchildren preparing rhubarb pie according to a
recipe she's never tried before

He rises slightly in the air
at the ad for the new vampire movie

She doesn't notice his black cape and
momentary fangs yellow eyes and angular glances
she's ministering to impoverished children in

Rwanda wrapping bundles and patting foreheads
having developed the serum that will wipe out the virus forever

Neither have left their chairs
neither have spoken to each other for over an hour

They button their coats and get up from the table
the newspapers are left behind folded neatly to one side

The world stays exactly as it was from one moment to the next

Nothing stays the same

1/2

HE SAW THE WAY THE WORLD

He saw the way the world makes a sharp turn just
around the curve ahead and disappears
even as he runs to catch it or stealthily
tiptoes along as if to
sneak up on it

like an unruly child like a Grecian sylph on a
Keatsian vase it's always one step ahead of us to
elude our grasp

The world puffs to smoke as we grab it
the smoke makes ghoulish faces in the light
all the careful buttons we once buttoned
come undone
as well as the laces nails screws smiles levers song
all the things we've come up with to
forestall its disappearance

But it was always ephemeral we should have
noted and remembered
from embryonic first cramped quarters
to later perhaps more spacious apartments with views

Like a perfect crystal swan swathed in flame gliding
unperturbed it doesn't suddenly
wake up and flap its colossal wings when we
shout at it
it often turns to us a bland face even after all the
sizzling enthusiasms we've offered it even on the official

sacrificial china the plates with
family crest and filigreed gold leaf borders

ah, let it go

A green river will eventually grow over it

It might even one day transform into pure music
a tune we can try to recall for
nostalgic reasons at least
and sing to ourselves to remind ourselves of

the worlds' and our
own selves' passing nature

in the star-spangled night

1/9

HE SAW WITH CRYSTAL GAZES

He saw with crystal gazes
the place he was meant to inhabit

its porphyry goblets and marble chairs
hillsides dotted with illumined sheep

scarlet river like a gash through the mountains
forests of every species of tree in every

available natural grove
animals of every species roaming at their own sweet wills

canoes down silvery waterways going where they may
lakes covered with water birds of every species

insects of every species purposefully
crisscrossing the ground in search of whatever each

species needs to survive
and he saw the crowded world he lived in with its

crisscross of busy streets and unnatural congestion
noise not of cracking branches underfoot on a

silent day where a falling leaf is noticed
but the chords and threnodies of

buses and taxis
and smoke of concrete geometry in

distorted dimensions
and he turned the telescope around

and deer streamed between the cavalcades and
Mardi Gras of multi-colored distractions

rain crystals in elongated shapes rained down onto
paved streets suddenly themselves crystallized

everything shimmered in
vibrating harmony each jagged edge cunningly

fitting seamlessly into air's grooves and
matter's accommodating corners somehow

and he saw where he was meant to inhabit was where
he was right now

on a rising geyser-spout of light
reverberating everywhere

to say nothing of the various other vagrants
equally appropriately placed here and

equally perplexed

1/10

GHAZAL OF THE ROSE

The most difficult rose is the rose that needs to be picked
or we could say the simple rose is the most difficult rose to be picked

The complication in this matter really resides with us
and not with the one that is the one that is the most to be picked

But rather which rose out of the sea of the entire rose bed
is most likely out of the free choice of these or those to be picked

And by a rose of course I mean a complex metaphor
plucked from out of the metaphorical wind that blows to be picked

A beauty that seems to circle round and round itself in
delicate deep dark petals and velvety folds to be picked

One where God's breath seems to have been freshly breathed
on this glorious creation of His that looks as if it knows to be picked

Not that easy weed or that gaudy flower over there
but the regal thorn-protected citadel worthy of Moses to be picked

So fresh and gloriously swirling its frond-like petals
with deepest secrets of light we must be metamorphosed to be picked

Is it a rose even? Or is it a knowledge in the heart
that opens in an ever more pulsing river that flows to be picked

And is it God's city in fact of radiant purity
in the shape of a flower on a stem that grows to be picked?

I wonder if I shall ever see it in my own lifetime
for it's a rare bloom in a rarer garden laid out in geometrical rows
     to be picked

And once our hand reaches the stem and we gaze deep in
we must say goodbye to this world and *"peace"* to the one we
     chose to be picked

Freed into space from within and completely at ease from without
in the sense that now we've become God's own sweet-smelling
     rose to be picked

That we ourselves so yearned for year after year and moment after
     moment
our own breaths in remembering billows to be picked

O God let that rose that arose in our hearts at birth
by Your love be the one our whole life hurries and slows to be picked

And let it be placed from Your Garden into the receptacle You've
     given us
whose mouth stays open in eternity even as our own life closes
     to be picked

Until You breathe the sweetness of our budding bloom
and Your own scent fills our actual physical nose to be picked

out from all life's possible scents in this world
and may we always choose your single most crystalline and sublime
     rose to be picked

1/16

SAINT FRANCIS STOOD

for Ned O'Gorman

Saint Francis stood in the same spot until he was stone
now it was the poppies that bled
it was the air that ached
it was the sky that beseeched clemency

His eyes were fixed on the horizon of light within the horizon
though the sheep and the gnarled olive trees
felt the same as always
now they had blue lightning coursing through their souls
and even the dullest stones on the road were part of the
divine mosaic

Saint Francis became bread birds pecked from
he became puddles for bugs and mud for worms
his words were lost in the sung choirs of his actions
in a hand held out to another hand
naked babies leapt forth from his womb into the shining sun

He turned to go humming softly to himself
and the hills settled back into being hills
sheep and olive trees bugs and worms and birds
browsed waved branches tiptoed oozed and
flew along through the sky as usual
a little lighter to his tune

1/22

A BED

A bed
a not particularly distinguished bed though we
might put a Louis XVI headboard on it to
give it some grandeur a mahogany affair with
little pillars and carved cupids say

Bed of conception with huge petal-like lily white sheets wildly strewn

Bed of birth with those same sheets now blood-soaked and the
room in a different kind of psycho-physiological uproar

Bed of the wounded and here it could
just as well be one of those dilapidated canvas cots enough to
accommodate a grimacing victim awaiting Civil War amputation with a
rusty nail between his teeth for anesthesia and
Walt Whitman at his side holding his hand and caressing his brow

Bed of penance hard as marble cold and severe

Bed of commerce in a back-street backroom in Singapore with the sound of
passing bicycles tinkling by leaving trails of cigarette smoke

Worldwide bed in a yurt snow blowing a gale outside in a remote
region in Outer Mongolia
horsehair mattress with two or three
kelims of awesome weave and deep rich red and green earth tones
thrown haphazardly across it

Bed of Eskimos carved out of ice blocks

Bed of Tuaregs heaped up sand and a few extravagant pillows

Bed of pressed pine needles under a doe giving
birth to a fawn in a forest as quiet as a velvet glove being
pulled on by a nun in a cathedral in Trieste

Bed elevated or lowered for the lifelong invalid with the
crystal clear mind unbeknownst to everyone

Last bed of Napoleon at St. Helena with stained curtains no bigger than a
zinc bathtub like the one Marat was
stabbed to death in

Then finally
beds of death since the beginning of time to
my own wherever it may be if it's actually a bed
in a room with shades drawn and a few
shadowy loved ones gathered in the gloom
the Face of God Himself hovering at last with
benign waterfall rock-face celestial avalanche pouring
majestically upward to the
sound of faraway xylophones and etherial voices of soft bells

Bed of silence in a world of noise

Deathbed of length so lengthy it actually
extends into the next world

he thinks to himself tending his roses
leaning down getting snagged momentarily by a thorn
bleeding bright red blood a few perfect

drops onto the
bare ground of his rose bed

1/23

THE TREASURE

The treasure in the dungeon by the wall
under the long stone stairs dripping with water
by the barred window looking out on the
tropical seacoast seven floors down
under ground level through winding blind
corridors arrived at past dark sentries in
chain mail with maces standing stiffly at attention
through an archway hidden and all but
totally obscured by thick drapery on a top floor
achievable by a small stairway at the
far end of a dank chamber off the
main hall otherwise unknown except by
those with prior knowledge or a
map inside the huge fortress surrounded by a
murk-filled reflectionless moat inhabited by poisonous biting
sea-creatures on a distant island off the
unbeaten sea-path between two totally
obscure and barren land masses torn
constantly by storms day and night and
howling winds and high snarling surf
ceaselessly

is the heart
filled with light
the universe turned completely inside out inside it
at one with every living atom
whispering His Name

1/24

OUR HEARTS LIKE FRESH LOAVES OF BREAD

Our hearts like fresh loaves of bread just out of the oven
set on windowsills between our selves and the world
thieves abound just outside on the street ready to run off with them
school children passing by under the window in their
starched school uniforms luxuriate in their wafting odors floating past their
noses and realize just how hungry they are
strangers and friends alike admire their color and texture
the resilience and buttery crustiness of their crusts
while we watch over the loaves from within against squirrels and
wild birds to make sure
no one snatches them off the sill or knocks them to the
ground through sheer clumsiness

as they cool and mature to the point that they can be
taken inside and set on checkerboard table-cloth'd tables
(this world made of opposites black and white)
with a little virgin olive oil and a sharp knife
(the knife say that distinguishes between divine love and lusty passion)

and this belabored metaphor at last sliced right down the
middle into two halves with a prayer that
both halves go to heaven

the heart made whole in a savory unity
the taste of its zesty essence
become pure nourishment for all

1/25

LITTLE GOLDEN HANDS

Little golden hands are playing a billion molecular pianos
up and down the scales through phyla flora and fauna of
everything oblivious to time but rhythmically thumping time's
boat-hull as it crashes through eternity's breakers
each one higher than the Empire State Building
licking against heaven then
curling down again into the general brine
that sizzles into a momentary silence so long whole
universes bathe for centuries in its stasis and so short the blip is
hardly experienced by anything but a little
interrupted starlight in some distant corner galaxy that was
already distracted by the gorgeous coming-to-birth of a flaming
red color against a
burgundy cobalt background streaked with mercurial silver
in this universe of concentration and distraction
multiplication and subtraction in which
nothing is ever added to or divided from or shifted
in your smile or glint of eye like creased velvet
like crumpled foil splashed with amber
without those little golden hands playing a
tune so catchy and memorable in the
everyday reality of filthy subway entrances or
soot in the air with a divine face flashing in it for an
instant before falling everywhere at once
over everything in singable and melodious tones

1/28

HE GETS A POSTCARD

He gets a postcard from the next world
perfectly blank

but in a certain light he can see
domes and groves of trees and circular paths

and hear its uncanny music
and taste its heavenly tastes

and it is enough to keep him going for him
to look at it from time to time as it

sits in its silver spotlight
radiating imageless splendor

and the scent in the air where it sits
is different from where it isn't

the way a rose in its place presents a
perfume that isn't anywhere else but there

yet it is more like a hole in space
than an actual object

a hole of even indeterminate size
through which he can see eternity

which looks very much the same as here
but from a different standpoint

presided over by the same Presence
with golden touch but invisible fingers

whose smile without lips can be seen floating
on both sides at once over everything

He picks up the postcard and puts it in his pocket
and sails out the door on a utilitarian errand

Halfway there he is visited by a light
sent by the postcard's signator

and disappears without a trace
though he may be sitting next to us

each with a postcard in our pocket from the next world
perfuming the place we are in the way a rose does

unobtrusively beautiful
transforming us into rose-scent

2/6

THE EGYPT SERIES

1

Alligator diplomats and crocodile bibliophiles
unite in their enthusiasm to make the traveler

feel welcome

as he alights in pith helmet and archeological gear
with box camera folded in his wind-proof canvas bag

interior intentions well-established beforehand
in whatever doily-covered parlor he set out from

around maps and sextants calipers and very slim
eraserless pencils with a grunting grand uncle who'd

been to Egypt before just after Napoleon carted off
the Rosetta Stone and the Sphinx's nose to a

damp warehouse in some *arondissement* or other

2

We travel to die
Close the door and
lock it on drawers filled with kewpie dolls
closets of clown suits bird cages filled with
partridges and singing canaries suites of mismatched

furniture and drapes of uncarded lambs' wool hanging like hair
maps left unrolled on polished mahogany tables
ghosts in single file up vaporous escalators to nowhere
family trees whose last and ripest fruit dangling
dangerously over the abyss is suddenly
us

stepping aboard space flight number one to a vague destination
through hallway
mirrors that are not even this world whose fleeting
glimpses show nude beaches and market stalls with
eyecatching shawls and oriental carpets

though none really exist in this place of icicle
mental winds and solar coronary flares across even the
tiniest momentary distraction from the
perfect goal whose attribute beyond all attribution

is perfection itself in the moisture
of an eye
and the thankfulness of the tongue before
His Imperishable Presence

3

People really do speak different languages I
think to myself sitting in the Zurich airport on my
way to Cairo

God really did confound mankind's tongues

at that tower's inexpressible height

though most of the vowels and consonants are the
same with a few guttural twists and glottal
twangs and slim *umlaut* carvings of vowels

and yet everyone somehow communicates
and I often wonder at tender words between
lovers in Siamese or mystical Mongolians
speaking to their God in beseeching terms

and what if we all were struck blind and had to
negotiate through language alone to apprehend the
subtlest meanings often conveyed with a
wink a smirk a shrug

or were all struck mute instead
and had to communicate with winks and
smirks shrugs and hand gestures whose
constants from ethnic group to ethnic group were only
four fingers and a thumb

4

He alights from a groaning camel in front of the
inscrutable entrance to the imponderable but somehow
imperishable pyramid over whose apex a
hawk shadow flies plus many fuzzy godly
afterimages filing through the sky of animal-headed
figures all walking sideways

and he sniffs in the preemptory way certain
adventurers and explorers have of sniffing which is one part
actually smelling out the situation and one part
a kind of proprietary arrogance as if after
eons of belonging to someone else this foreign interloper who is
much more expert than anyone so far
is here to take charge

Alabaster gargoyles silver chased with lapis and ruby
scepters up against walls of gold with so far undeciphered
whispered messages in pure pictograph
cloth about to dissolve like gossamer once worn a few
centuries ago by slender actual maidens in ripe actual
weather now gone into the pure abstract of
time past and taking its live specimens with it

But he's alive now and alighted from a camel
walks up to the deep entrance shadowed from the high
Giza sun and sniffs once or twice and
clears his throat and makes a little grunting camel noise
and peers into the darkness

5

The rose is a door but you do not knock
its thorns are a knob but you do not grasp

the sun is a house whose heat is love
the door is a flame but you stay in the shade

the wheel of death's engine is rolling your way
its rim is its axel its core is its tire

the eye you see with is a wrong-way telescope
so what is vast becomes as miniscule as salt-grains

you have taken a path just big enough for two feet
yet you think it's the world and it's not even a side street

what's before you is within you and what's within you is before you
but you still mistake the smile that slays for the knife that saves

what's in front of you is behind you and what's above you is below you
but you insist on rolling with the punches when you should be

singing praises

It's time to come clean for once and call out all your nefarious
accomplices

put sacks on their heads and strings tight round their necks and send
them all home

it's a mountain of ice at birth and our life melts it as it goes
the ice water is up to our knees already yet we still stubbornly resist

6

A lithe leopard leaps to a ledge
and looks down at him

Is he really all alone? *What luck!*

An ibex blinks but only in beatitude
three scorpions with a procession of sweet scorpion
babies scuttle in T. S. Eliot fashion across the
desert floor in the sizzling sun
hawks dip and swerve and
all this continues to occur as he peers in at the
black entrance not quite sure how to
proceed though the leopard with the slightly
human face might have a few culinary
suggestions

He pokes with a stick and is greeted by a
hollow echo

He pushes forward while pushing his pith helmet
back on his head
scorpion babies click scorpion babies click-clicking along

He inches forward his entire scholarly career
hanging on the next few minutes as well as
Lady Haliburton's funding of the entire
expedition

He points his Victorian flashlight though apparently
batteries have been known for centuries such as those
mysterious lumpy ones from Syria or Iraq

It lights up a few yards in front of his
mustachio'd nose

which he follows inside
the entire pyramid swallowing him and by association a
part of the British Empire as well as if
sucking on a mint

7

I see past the ridge to the horizon where a
dozen blue roses bloom at the edge like
acetylene sparks
in a fine amber light where the lumber of dream gets
piled in a pyramid inside the starry night dome

where endlessly chewing camels of last
remnants of thought block the way
usually reserved for
stretches of emptiness

now crowded beyond measure with the
massive ratiocinations of actually nothing
at all if you don't count mortality as
part of the equation

like sand grains falling in front of sheer sheets of
falling water with a fine mist rising at
exactly the same ratio and golden canaries
singing perfect arias between the
strands

where a voice invisibly rings out the call to prayer in

Cairo before dawn answered by another
voice across town ringing out then

another then another like an aural tapestry falling from
Paradise freshly woven each thread ignited
with blue roses blooming at the edges

blue sparks scattering in the dark
and falling into dawn

8

He entered but what has he entered but the
essence of entering itself

body in a black hole pulled inward
anatomical shape framed by a nothingness rectangle

He breathes ancient dust motes
that attach themselves to his lung sacs

his eyes getting accustomed to the dark treacled aside slightly
by the yellowy beam of his flashlight

He moves forward from skeleton outward
ball of foot and toe-pads pushing against earth

looking wildly in front of him his whole
being intent on what's

in front of him that it stay perfectly still
millennially still for him to come upon and

inspect without sudden movement
though his imagination's running rampant

checking through various archeological journals
pulling out charts and diagrams in sepia

ink against crinkling cream-colored
parchment in his mind

He comes to a wall that's a door right in front of his nose
his heartbeats knock on it as loud as backfire but it's been

sealed for centuries

His heartbeats boom into the dark rectangle he's in
filling it past its perimeters

He reaches out to brush his fingertips against the
dried mud of it

in the millennial silence
first light swish sounds of human fingertips against wall

in that rectangle deep in the pyramid in the
pitch dark except for his wobbly light beam

in the early morning
with hot sunlight pouring down all around outside

and his donkey impatiently waiting
occasionally stamping the ground with its

hooves and occasionally snorting

2/8-25 *(Cairo and Fayyoum Egypt)*

NEWLY DISCOVERED GREEK FRAGMENT

Odysseus alias Ulysses ate an olive and
smacked his lips salaciously
high winds were blowing them homeward
he took out the pit and flung it leeward
also flung pits the first mate and steward

His starry eyes flashed and his ten fingers flexed
did Odysseus solicitously
"Who've you got home Ilkus —
kids?" few words between wind-swords
"Twelve" replied Ilkus and licked his thick lips
tickled with fleeciness
"Larboard! Larboard!" cried Lalopopolous laboriously
from somewhere to their left

Odysseus rose suddenly his upper trunk gloriously rosy
the ship lurched unlaughingly
lifted suddenly precariously dryward on a
giant fishback who
almost took care not to
shake them seaward though their state was less than
pleasing sung suddenly by seagulls as if
gull words would steady them

The ship's crew sat silent none screamed though their
eyes did
their mouths became tongueless and their
knuckles like knobs around oar-heads or
nothingness smooth and near circular

Odysseus' eyes now filled with tears compassionately flickering
seeing his men in such peril and so
close they were to home

"Oh fish!" he yelled *"Don't finish us! Oh
God!"* he howled *"Release us!"*

And the sea became salubrious
and the dangerous dastard disappeared almost as
quickly as it had surfaced and the crew all leaned now

forward sweat
glistening on their foreheads
Odysseus' eye-teeth also now glistening

"Thank God!" he said gratefully and relievedly
listening

3/1

THIS LOVE

l'amor che move il Sole e l'altre stelle
— Dante

This love that shaped the distant stars

and this rock here and the flat it's on and its
irregular shadow and the gnat that
lands on it briskly wipes its feelers and legs
together and then takes off into thin air

and that shaped the delicate curves of your lips
and the appreciation deep inside the sponge
folds of my brain I have for them noting their
arched beauty perched on your being like exotic birds

and this love unseen we're counting on to
pull us forward all the way to the end
and even pull us through when we have no more
will than a plank or this rock here with its
shadow in the shape of a sinister barrister a
flying squirrel a house on fire a lake of pure
soul-essence across which we might
swim to safety at last in love's rising light

This love that awaits us which is ninety-nine times more
powerful than any of the love we can
see here on earth between Creator and creature or
creature and creature or even
inert earth and creatures which is in itself a

realm of such electronic blessing even the
air itself we all breathe by the very
miracle of its breatheability

The love that calls us home and whose
echo rings through the deep rounds already closely
ringing inside us like answering chimes
or that actually begins from deep inside those coils as the
very origin of that call

like a flock of white flying birds who
turn in the sun and seem to disappear then
suddenly seem to appear out of thin air again and it
turns out that all along they were there
but for a trick of the eye

This love that created the call and
that answers the call and that
walks in between both answer and call with our

faces always facing and never really
turning away from it

This love that moves the sun and the other stars

3/8

AT THE POINT

At the point of being torn apart by wolves
or eaten by tigers
I wonder if you find yourself on a
high plateau at a little silver table say
eating grapes out of a cut glass bowl
or on a windy plain holding the sides of your
coat as you watch distant fire leap from
treetop to treetop

If as the shark closes razor teeth on your
arm or neck or as you
sail down past floor after floor of city
skyscraper you might find yourself on
horseback at a gallop through seasurf on a
bright sunny afternoon in Majorca heading for the
chateau on the hill for paella and tea

God's mercy exceeds His wrath
His delicacy exceeds His ferocity
each soul's comfort is somehow
assured as the axe falls and *"God be praised!"*
leaves the lips of the
soon-to-be-beheaded nobleman or highwayman
in whose eyes a sudden Technicolor Paradise has
just been displayed where soft green hills lead to
gently gurgling streams as the pollen-laden air hits his
eyelids going down on a scene that will soon be
more real than this one with its
crashing timbers and atomic structures fraying at their

tenuous threads and sifting into
heaps of lint behind the incautious
furniture of this world

3/9

LOVERS REUNITED

Lovers reunited after years of separation
never mind why
don't notice the pin stripes or polka dots of their
very physical reunion they see
the high wind in the other's eyes or the conch-shell
pearlescence or something about the mouth opening to
speak that resembles the noble height of
Victoria Falls when herons have just passed
through the water strands
and the jungle noise all around
has settled down to a virginal silence

Blue or brown in the shapes of this world
tight or loose high or low all the relative approximations to
perfection evaporate in the light of the
fire of love's recognitions
which sees through appearances to the volcanic center
out of whose molten core spring
glass harps playing our song in extended
arpeggios so intricately vast none of the
notes have time to decay in the air until the
space all around as well
lights up in pure sound

3/15

A GALAXY FLUNG

A galaxy flung like a fiery jump-rope into the sky
where it glitters among stars slowly twisting and changing shape

A white bear on a white ice floe in a bleached arctic fog
passing slowly under the arch of the sky like a single star

A pinpoint of light that lands on a
forehead or above the heart and sinks in
illuminating the whole inner being like a
dark tunnel flooded with headlights

The perfect enunciation of the word that opens
doors all down the soul's corridors each onto a
room in which the alchemy's taken place
and four-dimensional celebrations are in such full swing
invisible somersaults and handstands with ribbons of celestial music
in slow motion unfurl their satiny curls

I stand up in the heart's light to sing this song
and knock the roof off the house
and topple the mockingbird off the television aerial
who stops for a moment regroups then takes up where it
left off with hardly a pause and never a
faulty note

The clock is ticking into this inventory like a
train bound for Natchez filled with
inflammable cargo
our identities on this earth and all our

desperate presumptions
when space within space in various shapes open to the
endlessly changing panorama that goes beyond
death at the beginning and
birth at the end or vice-versa
God's fingerprints all over us like a celestial crime-scene

is our rightful condition

and our endlessly spontaneous full-throated
proclamations of praise

3/16

THE HARPIST

for W.A. Mathieu

The harpist grows old plucking the
multicolored strings of his harp

yet he never gets tired of harping
for white steeds are always

galloping full-tilt out of the walls across a
sunlit courtyard fresh from distant stretches

or a leaf falls from high up on a
cypress and twists in slow spirals to its destined spot on an

irregular flagstone or Jacosta stabs herself
with a naturally honed icicle or a baby is

held up in both lights to the Glory of God
the sun and moon which each day shine

for the first time
and the harpist whose hands are

veins of celestial straws full of blood from the life-source
plucks the songs of all these orbiting scintillations

and his face cools and his eyelids glow and his
lips move to such bell-clear plucking

suspending notes from the taut staves of silence
and his shoulders roll like breakers

and the harp itself changes dimension and becomes a
million harps up mirrored staircases also in a

spiral turning slowly around a single axis
yet the harpist remains one though his

face varies and his fingers are
pages in a dictionary fluttering through all the

vocal possibilities branching from
the dark quiet of ancient roots

whose glottis like a harp note sounds and
vibrates and can be heard in this world

though its harpist actually is reaching through
from the next

3/21

THE GREEN FIRES

"The green fires" was what came to me in the
middle of the night last night and I
diligently wrote it down at the
top of this page fully expecting a poem of some
worth to follow by suggesting further
lines sinking or rising to an exhilarating
conclusion though no real
conclusion be possible yet there might be
yawning gulfs full of roses each with a
distinctive scent to activate the reptile brain or
whatever to concatenate a happy verbal sequence
or else there's nothing but the yawn then
back to sleep but I can soon tell if
spirit voices under the silence are lightly
knocking on the lid to be let out

And then it's golden canoes down wide green Savannah floods
skimming all the way to Memphis
or the flight of toucans and other nearly extinct birds from far or
near endangered trees through an air that is also
almost gone until they make their
eternal reappearance in the poem
as noiseless as spiders they
fly through the blue of words to an
unknown destination leaving
wing-prints on the page for decipherers to
decipher

and *"the green fires"* sat by itself uncontinued for a

day on the page until now when I don't
dive into it in the usual way with pen and
mental snorkel firmly in place but rather
take off from its failure to mature and
flower into its own poem making instead this
poem about my mode of composition of poems
which may in fact have to do with the combustible
freshness of *"green fires"* after all

3/26

EVERYTHING MOVES

Everything moves with a click into
place and a new configuration

You can't say if *this* had happened
that wouldn't have happened

river or coil flash increments in interlocking
pieces or overlays
forward or backwards or shivering from
side to side with elements coming
into the picture as integral
parts of the picture as much as a soul is
and from as far away as Alpha Centauri
and from as close in as deep inside a subatomic particle if
such exists in such splendid isolation

The death of someone by a series of seeming
accidents car avoiding donkey-cart careening into ditch
then unconsciousness coma and a day later
death

Take away any element and it doesn't come into play
and the person who dies drives on to another
assemblage another interlocking of essential
elements tainted mushroom that killed the
Buddha poisoned meat that
killed the Messenger of God
head on a platter as Salomé herself moves
inescapably forward to her own intricately

designed encounter with the delicate
machinery of mortality cogs and levers

made of Rilke's rose-thorn or Mussolini's
maddened crowd

I sit between a purring cat and a ticking clock
hunched over this notebook
about to more forward into my day

3/27

THE LAST TIME

The last time someone came through here
brandishing a too-small chair at a
too-huge lion
the night declined to settle down among the
rest of the furniture
and in the morning the lawn sprinklers found
cactuses grown up like weeds

"It's a matter of scale" someone said
when faced with eternity you don't consult a
stopwatch
when faced with mortality you don't hold out
a bus ticket
when faced with your self after all these
years playing the same part with a
limited number of the same props
you don't hold out your own sad self as
ransom in hopes of exchanging it for a
similar one with more youthful complexion

What looks like a sky isn't the back of a
truck like a wide-load concrete wall making its
slow way down the highway

What looks like stars isn't
troops of children on hilltops with laser flashlights
hoping for Some Mores

What you hold up is a key made of ice that

perfectly fits a fiery lock
but once it's inserted the key is lost and the
door burns entirely away

Some immensities won't be seduced into
words and some
perceptions are actually so far beyond our
apparatuses of perception that only the
heart – God's lodging – has space and
time adequate to the job

Only a wind in place of a person a
sunrise and its clear arc into sunset

Only a sound like a gong whose
vertical lake of reverberations extends to the
edges of the world
can be called a true one

and an encompassing lion

and a nothing

and a simple light

3/28

THE SUBTLEST NOTES OF THE CALL

May the monkey on your back become a stallion
as it slithers down your body to become
your steed of travel
planted firmly under you so you can
ride it to the Land of Glory
(sounds like a gospel song)

May all the psychic tics and tremors
that earthquake what is stable in you into
shifting parts with deep gulfs between each one
become a smooth dance step instead like
say a tango to soft accordion music

May all the ice storms and sleet falls of
chill isolation in the world from
everyone your own hearts' gyroscope
the Holy Presence itself in fact become
cool trickles down the sides of a tropical joy where the
thick air laden with fruit sweetness
unites the way oceans unite the continents they thrash around
the flying elements of your being into one
deliriously endurable crescendo

May your heart alight forever in the
upper boughs of the tree for more
intimate moon-viewing

and may your ears be ever more finely attuned to hear
through walls thicker than life itself

the subtlest notes of the call

4/3-4

LIQUIDLY AUDACIOUS

Liquidly audacious as a Sicilian summer
or the bright blue long-gone feet of a Hindu god
or like a shadow that slips in when you're least aware
and suddenly there are three where there were only two
or some more complex multiplication of the original integer

yet as sinewy as a mist above a mountain trail
going to the peak and overlooking the
Valley of Lost Souls over on your left *The Plain of The Supreme Test*
there in the middle foreground and *The Plateau of
Divine Reprieve and Eternal Happiness* on your far right
with soft showers of a very pale coral rain falling on
laughing faces and rambunctious wolverines

or as blunt as time itself in the way it
imposes a pinnacle surrounded by native huts
where before there was only the tangly stomping ground of egrets
or the inexorable aging process so that no matter how
incorrigibly positive the soul is all around it
the body sags and aches and tries to bring the
spirit with it and almost pulls it off except that
golden horses the size of spouting hydrants keep pulsing
forward out of an almost overlooked ditch
whinnying *Glory Halleluiahs!* to make even the most
staunch skeptic smile

and as tall as the sky itself that keeps on going without
letup until it gets darker and darker like a closet full of
black winter coats and discarded gift boxes and darker and darker

until there is only darkness and floating in a dimensionless darkness
and you think this is where death goes after all
or this is where death comes from this
completely compatible darkness but then there's a

glimmer and a fading and a gradual melting of the
darkness out in space and you find you're nearing a
neighboring galaxy like a sizzle of minute sparks of
light running its fringe along the
outermost edge of such an absolute deathly darkness and soon you're
floating in the proximity of planets with their
moons and Magellanic clouds and everything's as
distant as possible from your point of origin until you start to

recognize certain roofs and town configurations
and certain clearings of the mist away from yourself there
coming out to meet the voyaging stranger
and you see it's actually yourself after all
meeting your invisible half or actual unified totality
in a living moment

as liquidly audacious as a Sicilian summer as sinewy as a mist as
blunt as time itself and as tall as the sky
where before you thought you were just so-and-so alone in the universe
on such-and-such a street
gazing up at the moon on a frigid night and wondering
how it all began and when it would all end

as a trickle of water from the infinite ocean of air above and all around you
falls in the distance on a flat rock making a gentle
plink sound and then the sound of the pulling away of a

car from a curb and a
vaguely delicious smell of cooking with hot sauce and
peppermint cumin and oregano

and someone just over the fence next door
starts singing off key in a
cracked voice that like a
lost squirrel in snow is deeply
poignant nevertheless

THE MOTOR RUNNING

Three drops from the ocean of love fell on the
hem of my shirt

though I could hear its crashing surf far above both the
stars and the liquid daylight

and it crashed on the earth like hands slapping
dough to be made into bread

or like a whisper in a room so silent
everyone can hear

Three drops alone reached me but I'm now
helplessly drunk since the sender of these

drops though coquettish is made real by the
moisture and shape of the drops

one drop for loyalty one drop for eternity and the
last one for death whose car door is always

open and the motor running

4/7

A BREATH OF FRESH AIR

A breath of fresh air
sailed over the highest mountain peak and
down into the valley enjoying its
nonchalant pace over grassy plains as
green as unripe apples and the

breath of fresh air turned with the prevailing
current through a massive gorge and
just above a river where tumultuous waters as they
hurled over rocks resembled storm clouds though no
storm was brewing and the

breath of fresh air saw a city ahead and
pulled itself tighter though no less fresh
as it looped in a little air-pocket for a
short while which slowed its pace and
gave it some rest so that when it

began again toward the city it was going at a
much more leisurely rate and could really
take its time over outlying fields and across
meandering herds of sheep and goats that never even
looked up to see the fresh breath of air pass overhead

and the breath of fresh air descended slowly as it
passed the first thatched cottages dotted almost
haphazardly along the hills and it
skimmed along their brown roofs and lifted a
little as it headed toward a more concentrated

cluster of buildings and streets and now some
converging streets down below and traffic and even
noise like its memory of ocean surf

and the breath of fresh air pulled itself more
tightly together over children's playgrounds and
a group of people sitting and eating under a
tree which the breath of fresh air slowly
circulated around admiring the massive
trunk filtering past each shapely leaf

and the breath of fresh air from the icy peak in the
far distance over the horizon finally sailed through an
open window in a tallish building with
green shutters where a sweet maiden was
sitting at a computer growing drowsy after a
long morning typing statistics
and as she turned her head and yawned
the breath of fresh air sailed happily into her
mouth and down her throat into her
filigreed lungs and she didn't know why exactly
maybe it was the mystery of yawning
but she suddenly felt
uncannily refreshed

and her topaz colored eyes glittered for a
moment almost seeing the last few
rivering miles of movement the

breath of fresh air had taken to its
momentary dark destination in her blood

4/8

THE FORTY-FOUR PERFECT ALABASTER TULIPS

Once out of nature I shall never take
My bodily form from any natural thing
— Yeats

The forty-four perfect alabaster tulips on your
right over there on their fragile stems and you can
hold them up to the light and see
mineral veins as the bulbs glow with an almost
supernatural light

as opposed to the dozen or so natural tulips there on your
left which glisten in the sunlight but yes are
subject to the air's ultimate bruising and must
drink water up their central straws to survive
and will turn brown and dry and droop and be
thrown away

I think I'm dying of various
diseases some more
ultimate than others with itches or rashes or
aches in odd places

and scribble in notebooks to establish I suppose
a certain alabaster luster an alabaster resilience
not to get thrown on top of frozen food packages in the
dark of some garbage can

Those forty-four alabaster tulips inert and unyielding

somehow gain from being with forty-three others
while one real tulip somehow has the whole
universe inside it

The real tulips can sink back into the
earth in the rank stink of death and dissolve into
worm-lettuce or just enzyme-mulch in that great circular
Ferris wheel of the elements that puts what's
deep down on top then after a complete revolution
back down on the bottom again

Well yes the body dies but may
God grant eternity to the eternal part in the
full glory of its flowering past both natural and alabaster
into His Supra-real realm of pure supernatural light

4/10

UP IN THE AIR (CONTINUING THE EGYPT SERIES)

Up in the air over the Atlantic Ocean on our way to
London I suddenly wonder what the
man I left at the black door to the
pyramid found

if he found as he went into the blackness
the past of the past
the ever-lengthening distance between what
actually did happen those many millennia ago
and his dusty foot-treads of now as he flashes his
bulbous flashlight into the dark

Things against walls walls against walls walls behind
walls between us and Reality it seems

even though I'm aloft in a British Airways airplane
wondering if he saw golden dust on a mummy's eyelash
or the words of the curse against intruders projected into
the space above the casket
those hieroglyphics animated and walking sideways in
single file to spell out by their kind of
Gurdjieffian movements the description of Ultimate Things
how chlorophyll works why some die why some live
what is the mystery of Glory that illuminates the
hearts of some souls while other souls are
left in darkness

I slit my eyes to gaze in through the emerald forest
to see how flame jumps from tree to tree

and how creatures flee disaster

A hill goes down to a lake of purifying water
legions of people in white clothes line up to wash in it
they're hungry and war-torn
they put their hands in the water and cup a
portion of it to their mouths
as they drink green butterflies chase purple ones
and the light from above turns golden

He staggers through the low-ceiling'd corridor
knocking over amphora overcome by the stale air and the
curiously sour stench of antiquity
he falls forward through faces that come to
meet him murmuring their names
he's never heard so many crazy names
the Embalmer the Lung-Remover the Canopic Jar Carver
the daughter of the Canopic Jar Carver
the man who carved the alabaster out of the
rock for the Canopic Jar Carver to carve

He saw a white flame and a green flame coiled in a
slowly turning wheel

He saw the invention of the toothbrush
the first fly swatter the look on the face of the
first woman to taste a perfect strawberry
baby's breath on a mirror to prove it was still alive
the past of the past and the momentary future

and the pyramid's doorway passed through him

on its way to eternity feeling the embrace of his
bones and the light in his eyes which
flashed as the flashlight burned out at last
leaving him at the center point of all light

We're halfway to London by the computer screen on the
seat-back in front of me
following a red arc above deep blue water
with two hours and fifty-five minutes to go

and the pyramid door passing through all of us
asleep in our chairs

4/11

A LIFE

The shower of light that he saw above the trees that day
and every day thereafter to the end of his
days whenever he lifted his eyes
the clicking sound as plants grew and the long
groaning sound of roots as they pushed downward
and the way sentences of deepest thought
voiced themselves in peoples' facial expressions so that he
always knew what people were thinking
underneath what they were saying

and his way of walking out of the space he was in
into a new space he would soon walk out of
but while inhabiting that chunk of space he would
do whatever was needed to be done in it
for the betterment of the world even if only
removing a hair or adding one small element to a
pattern where a crucial element was missing

And then came death and death's orchestra
with an emphasis on the low notes and the
amorphousness of its tunes
but he brought his own sheet music with him
and pretty soon they were playing a complex
song of praise everyone could sing
and did
as he lifted his hand just lightly
and swayed it to the appropriate rhythm

4/16

THE PARACHUTE

The parachute refused to open but he
never lost hope

the clouds went by much faster than they should have
and the fish went by much more slowly as he
sank to the level he was meant to in terms of
earthly existence and a life if not of crime at least of
breathing

and a liquid dance floor of dolphins dressed in formal gray and
black with white trim
and shadowy figures passing by near enough to have a
look at him as he made his way to a
satisfactory open space in a rhythm in harmony with the
rest of the floating folk here in the
middle of the ocean in the middle of
nowhere but he never lost hope on
land or on sea nor in the air as most
recently no he

kept his eyes wide open to assess the realities of
Reality as it revealed itself in flexible
stages like the stop photography of an orchid showing its
first peepings in its necklace of stem and
leaves to its pushing up and forth of velvety
petals then dangling its face-like flower with
spidery tongue and deep purple interior in the
momentary suspension of its beauty

which was how he saw this most radical tangent his
life had just taken allowing him little time for
reflection (or genuflection) but perhaps an
eternity of appreciation nevertheless of where his
Creator had placed him and was
continuing to place him face to face with a
situation both impossible and pure

and that he continues to the *n'th* degree to endure

4/18

THERE ARE POEMS ABOUT ROSES

There are poems about roses blooming on rose-stems
rising and swaying in an air of delirious voices

Love Lord is the fertile earth Your rich compost
black soil of death and disaffiliation that
precedes growth

black soil so rich in its blackness it gives
birth without effort

rose-songs lines of light new people walking out of
old people in endless single file

These rose-stems of love now have roses on them where before
only sky pregnant with rain heavily weighing down
the earth we walk on in hopes of running into
rose-beds tended by true lovers and heart people

willing to get snagged by their thorns to the point of
spilling precious blood-drops out of love

onto the black soil of the rose-bed

4/29

WHERE DEATH GOES

Where death goes for solace when no one's looking
in a spray of yellow parrot feathers
in the gnashed teeth of foxes

Where death goes after the lights are turned out
in the mortuary and the stillness expands to the
walls and laps against the closed doors

Where death goes in the eyesockets and throats of
young soldiers with their hands and arms flung back
just as they fell

death in the crinkle and the crack
in the crease and the winking clock

in the space in the dark between things left
behind where no insect or dust mote dare go

Where death goes after it's made its final declaration
its lone messenger withdraws to neutral ground
its many ministers and negotiators take late flights home

imponderable its appearance imponderable its
disappearance yet
some wear it bravely even brightly on their brows
while some seem fearfully to look in all the old familiar places
for a sign of its impending visit

while others wait impatiently at the bottom of the stairs

with expectant faces for it to come

Yet death *goes*
and takes us with it
and leaves a Polaroid on an upturned glass
full of sunset glow for those left behind to
ponder

And sings a soft song
as it sinks below the horizon

5/1

ABOUT THE AUTHOR

Born in 1940 in Oakland, California, Daniel Abdal-Hayy Moore's first book of poems, *Dawn Visions*, was published by Lawrence Ferlinghetti of City Lights Books, San Francisco, in 1964, and the second in 1972, *Burnt Heart/Ode to the War Dead*. He created and directed *The Floating Lotus Magic Opera Company* in Berkeley, California in the late 60s, and presented two major productions, *The Walls Are Running Blood*, and *Bliss Apocalypse*. He became a Sufi Muslim in 1970, performed the Hajj in 1972, and lived and traveled throughout Morocco, Spain, Algeria and Nigeria, landing in California and publishing *The Desert is the Only Way Out*, and *Chronicles of Akhira* in the early 80s (Zilzal Press). Residing in Philadelphia since 1990, in 1996 he published *The Ramadan Sonnets* (Jusoor/City Lights), and in 2002, *The Blind Beekeeper* (Jusoor/Syracuse University Press). He has been the major editor for a number of works, including *The Burdah* of Shaykh Busiri, translated by Shaykh Hamza Yusuf, and the poetry of Palestinian poet, Mahmoud Darwish, translated by Munir Akash. He is also widely published on the worldwide web: *The American Muslim, DeenPort*, and his own website: www.danielmoorepoetry.com; and poetry blog: www.ecstaticxchange.wordpress.com, among others. He is also currently literary editor for *Seasons Journal* and *Islamica Magazine*. The Ecstatic Exchange Series is bringing out the extensive body of his works of poetry (a complete list of published works on page 2).

POETIC WORKS by Daniel Abdal-Hayy Moore
Published and Unpublished
(many to appear in The Ecstatic Exchange Series)

Dawn Visions (published by City Lights, 1964)
Burnt Heart/Ode to the War Dead (published by City Lights, 1972)
This Body of Black Light Gone Through the Diamond (printed by Fred
    Stone, Cambridge, Mass, 1965)
On The Streets at Night Alone (1965?)
All Hail the Surgical Lamp (1967)
States of Amazement (1970)

Abdallah Jones and the Disappearing-Dust Caper (published by The
    Ecstatic Exchange/Crescent Series, 2006)
The Chronicles of Akhira (1981) (published by Zilzal Press with
    Typoglyphs by Karl Kempton, 1986)
Mouloud (1984) (A Zilzal Press chapbook, 1995)
Man is the Crown of Creation (1984)
The Look of the Lion (1984)
The Desert is the Only Way Out (completed 4/21/84) (Zilzal Press
    chapbook, 1985)
Atomic Dance (1984) (am here books, 1988)
Outlandish Tales (1984)
Awake as Never Before (12/26/84) (Zilzal Press chapbook, 1993)
Glorious Intervals (1/1/85) (Zilzal Press chapbook, ?)
Long Days on Earth/Book I (1/28 – 8/30/85)
Long Days on Earth/Book II (Hayy Ibn Yaqzan)
Long Days on Earth/Book III (1/22/86)
Long Days on Earth/Book IV (1986)
The Ramadan Sonnets (Long Days on Earth/Book V) (5/9 – 6/11/86)
    (Published by Jusoor/City Lights Books, 1996) (Republished as
    Ramadan Sonnets by The Ecstatic Exchange, 2005)
Long Days on Earth/Book VI (6-8/30/86)
Holograms (9/4/86 – 3/26/87)
History of the World (The Epic of Man's Survival) (4/7 – 6/18/87)
Exploratory Odes (6/25 – 10/18/87)
The Man at the End of the World (11/11 – 12/10/87)
The Perfect Orchestra (3/30 – 7/25/88)

Fed from Underground Springs (7/30 – 11/23/88)
Ideas of the Heart (11/27/88 – 5/5/89)
New Poems (scattered poems, out of series, from 3/24 – 8/9/89)
Facing Mecca (5/16 – 11/11/89)
A Maddening Disregard for the Passage of Time (11/17/89 – 5/20/90)
The Heart Falls in Love with Visions of Perfection (6/15/90 – 6/2/91)
Like When You Wave at a Train and the Train Hoots Back at You (Farid's
    Book) (6/11 – 7/26/91) (Published by The Ecstatic Exchange, 2008)
Orpheus Meets Morpheus (8/1/91– 3/14/92)
The Puzzle (3/21/92 – 8/17/93)
The Greater Vehicle (10/17/93 – 4/30/94)
A Hundred Little 3-D Pictures (5/14/94 – 9/11/95)
The Angel Broadcast (9/29 – 12/17/95)
Mecca/Medina Time-Warp (12/19/95 – 1/6/96) (Published as a Zilzal
    Press chapbook, 1996)
Miracle Songs for the Millennium (1/20 – 10/16/96)
The Blind Beekeeper (11/15/96 – 5/30/97) (Published 2002 by Jusoor/
    Syracuse University Press)
Chants for the Beauty Feast (6/3 – 10/28/97)
You Open a Door and it's a Starry Night (10/29/97– 5/23/98)(Published by
    The Ecstatic Exchange, 2009)
Salt Prayers (5/29 – 10/24/98) (Published by The Ecstatic Exchange, 2005)
Some (10/25/98 – 4/25/99)
Flight to Egypt (5/1 – 5/16/99)
I Imagine a Lion (5/21 – 11/15/99)(Published by The Ecstatic Exchange, 2006)
Millennial Prognostications (11/25/99 – 2/2/2000)(Published by The Ecstatic
    Exchange, 2009)
Shaking the Quicksilver Pool (2/4 – 10/8/2000) (Published by The Ecstatic
    Exchange, 2009
Blood Songs (10/9/2000 – 4/3/2001)
The Music Space (4/10 – 9/16/2001) (Published by The Ecstatic Exchange,
    2007)
Where Death Goes (9/20/2001 – 5/1/2002) (published by The Ecstatic
    Exchange, 2009)
The Flame of Transformation Turns to Light (99 Ghazals Written in English)
    (5/14 – 8/21/2002) (Published by The Ecstatic Exchange, 2007)
Through Rose-Colored Glasses (7/22/2002 – 1/15/2003) (Published by The
    Ecstatic Exchange, 2008)

Psalms for the Broken-Hearted (1/22 – 5/25/2003) (Published by The Ecstatic Exchange, 2006)

Hoopoe's Argument (5/27 – 9/18/03)

Love is a Letter Burning in a High Wind (9/21 – 11/6/2003) (Published by The Ecstatic Exchange, 2006)

Laughing Buddha/Weeping Sufi (11/7/2003 – 1/10/2004) (Published by The Ecstatic Exchange, 2005)

Mars and Beyond (1/20 – 3/29/2004) (Published by The Ecstatic Exchange, 2005)

Underwater Galaxies (4/5 – 7/21/2004) (Published by The Ecstatic Exchange, 2007)

Cooked Oranges (7/23/2004 – 1/24/2005 (Published by The Ecstatic Exchange, 2007)

Holiday from the Perfect Crime (1/25 – 6/11/2005)

Stories Too Fiery to Sing Too Watery to Whisper (6/13 – 10/24/2005)

Coattails of the Saint (10/26/2005 – 5/10/2006) (Published by The Ecstatic Exchange, 2006)

In the Realm of Neither (5/14/2006 – 11/12/06)(Published by The Ecstatic Exchange, 2008)

Invention of the Wheel (11/13/06 – 6/10/07)

The Sound of Geese Over the House (6/15 –11/4/07)

The Fire Eater's Lunchbreak (11/10/07 – 5/19/2008) (Published by The Ecstatic Exchange, 2008)

Sparks Off the Main Strike (5/24/2008 – 1/10/2009)

www.ingramcontent.com/pod-product-compliance
Lightning Source LLC
Chambersburg PA
CBHW020908090426
42736CB00008B/533